THE
WEDDING NIGHT

Written By:
Ira Alterman &
Herbert Kavet

Illustrated By:
Martin Riskin

Manufactured in the United States of America

30 29 28 27 26 25 24 23 22 21 20 19 18 17 16 15 14 13 12 11 10 9 8 7 6 5 4 3 2 1

Ivory Tower Publishing Co., Inc.
125 Walnut St., P.O. Box 9132, Watertown, MA 02272-9132
Telephone #: (617) 923-1111   Fax #: (617) 923-8839

ARE YOU READY FOR ROMANCE?
A WEDDING NIGHT PREPAREDNESS TEST

For The Bride

Choose the answers which you think are correct, then see how ready for wedding night romance you are.

1. I believe the most important thing to get from your partner on your wedding night is:

a. Respect and understanding.
b. A good multiple orgasm.
c. The key to the handcuffs.
d. $50 a throw (I usually charge $100, but family is family).

A WEDDING NIGHT PREPAREDNESS TEST

2. If I think my partner is nervous, I would react by:

   a. Saying, "Look, honey, I'm nervous, too. Why don't we try to help each other."
   b. Saying, "Look, honey, I didn't bargain for a wimp. Come across, or else."
   c. Storming off to try and find a bellboy.
   d. Starting without him.

3. When your new husband says, "Why don't you slip into something more comfortable," is your first inclination to:

   a. Put on a sheer nightgown?
   b. Put on a flannel nightgown?
   c. Put on a sweatsuit?
   d. Put on some really comfortable hiking boots?

A WEDDING NIGHT PREPAREDNESS TEST

4. If your husband is being just a little too aggressive, would you:

   a. Say, "Take it easy, baby, we've got the rest of our lives?"
   b. Bounce your American Tourister off his forehead?
   c. Threaten to make him a eunuch?
   d. Make him a eunuch?

5. I only hope my husband:

   a. Is gentle and loving.
   b. Doesn't mind if I have a headache.
   c. Doesn't expect to get lucky on his first night.
   d. Has a strong back.

ARE YOU READY FOR ROMANCE?
A WEDDING NIGHT PREPAREDNESS TEST

For The Groom

Choose the answers which you think are correct, then see how ready for wedding night romance you are.

1. I believe the most important thing to get from your partner on your wedding night is:

    a. Respect and understanding.
    b. Your socks blown off.
    c. Fulfillment of a lifetime of sex fantasies.
    d. Wild applause.

A WEDDING NIGHT PREPAREDNESS TEST

2. If there was any one thing I would want my bride to know on our wedding night, it would be:

   a. That I love her.
   b. About my foot fetish.
   c. More positions than a hooker.
   d. How to make me crazy with her tongue.

3. I can't wait to be alone with my new bride on our wedding night so I can ask her:

   a. "Are you happy?"
   b. "Are you a virgin?"
   c. "Why did the desk clerk call you by your first name?"
   d. "Did you remember the olive oil and vanilla?"

A WEDDING NIGHT PREPAREDNESS TEST

4. I only hope my wife:

a. Thinks I am attractive.
b. Doesn't lock herself in the bathroom and scream like all the others.
c. Thinks my small penis is cute.
d. Doesn't expect to have an orgasm.

5. I know this sounds old-fashioned, but I believe in:

a. Getting to know each other slowly.
b. Going out the next day and bragging about how good I was.
c. The man being on top.
d. Asking the doorman to come up and comment on my technique.

WHAT EVERY BRIDE SHOULD KNOW ABOUT HER WEDDING NIGHT

8 KEY INDICATORS

Many brides ask, "How will I know if I'm in for a good time on my wedding night?"

That's a stupid question.

All they have to do is learn the 8 Key Indicators of a Good Wedding Night.

THE 8 KEY INDICATORS OF A GOOD WEDDING NIGHT

You know that you are going to have a good time on your wedding night if:

1. You walk into the bridal suite and trip over a case of condoms.

2. You sit on your husband's lap then realize he is standing up.

3. Your husband asks if you want to play a "get acquainted" game called "The Convict and the Milk Maid."

4. You get a beautiful silk nightgown with fur around the hem. The note in the box says, "To keep your neck warm."

THE 8 KEY INDICATORS OF A GOOD WEDDING NIGHT

5. You discover that someone has added a pair of knee pads to your trousseau.

6. You ask your husband why he is taking so much time in the bathroom and he says, "Because I'm doing my tongue exercises."

7. Two rough men appear at your bridal suite door carrying a glass slipper, a case of champagne, a tub of whipped cream, a large box marked, "Danger: Nuclear Vibrator," and six months of back copies of the magazine "German Shepherd Love."

8. You ask your husband why he is carrying a salami in his pajamas, and he says, "Salami? What salami?"

FIVE THINGS YOUR MOTHER NEVER TOLD YOU

The wedding night can be a beautiful, sensitive initiation into the arena of matrimonial bliss, or the devastating and humiliating near-disembowelment that has characterized wedding nights since the dawn of civilization. It all depends on how much you know.

FIVE THINGS YOUR MOTHER NEVER TOLD YOU

Most brides blunder into their wedding nights thinking: a) that they already know it all, or b) they are about to learn it all.

That is not enough. To truly prepare for your wedding night, you need to know five very important things about men, things that women have spent generations learning, things that your mother never told you.

FIVE THINGS YOUR MOTHER NEVER TOLD YOU

Here are things about men you had better be prepared for unless you want your wedding night to be the most traumatic and unhappy experience of your life (not counting the time you found out where babies really come from.)

1. Men are 2% aftershave, 3% libido and 95% body hair. And they shed like goats in rut. Don't be surprised if, after you've been married for seven minutes, your entire wardrobe is covered with your husband's body hair, and there is hair all over the bathroom and all over the sheets. The only way to eliminate the problem is to make your groom sleep in a Hefty bag.

FIVE THINGS YOUR MOTHER NEVER TOLD YOU

2. Men do not like to be touched after they've had an orgasm. It makes their skin crawl. Men like to curl up into a ball and go to sleep after they've had an orgasm, then get up when you are sleeping and jump on you and start all over again. Anything you've ever read about men making love to a woman more than one time in a row is a lie.

FIVE THINGS YOUR MOTHER NEVER TOLD YOU

3. Men like to think they are the first one. Even if they know they are not. They like to believe that, by some act of divine intervention, you have never done it with anyone else before. Lie to them and say it is so. Who could it hurt, even if you are in your third marriage?

FIVE THINGS YOUR MOTHER NEVER TOLD YOU

4. Men want to believe that you sleep in the nude because they sleep in the nude. Men sleep in the nude because they think it is a turn-on; with most men, it is not. So if your new husband asks if you sleep in the nude, be coy and say, "I've never had any reason to before." That will make him feel special, until he sees you in your flannel nightgown on the next night.

FIVE THINGS YOUR MOTHER NEVER TOLD YOU

5. Men expect their new wives to be both virgins and practiced in the art of exotic lovemaking. They especially like it if you know how to do things with pillows. Many a new bride has gotten her marriage off to a solid start by doing things with pillows on her wedding night. Many a new bride has gotten even on the second night by holding the pillows over her husband's face when he snores.

WHAT MEN THINK IF THEY ARE VIRGINS ON THEIR WEDDING NIGHT

Hey, this is just like jerking off, only you don't have to fantasize.

WHAT WOMEN THINK IF THEY ARE VIRGINS ON THEIR WEDDING NIGHT

Hey, this is just like playing with yourself, only you don't come.

WHY MEN HAVE MORE FUN ON THE WEDDING NIGHT

Men can come in
43 seconds and then
roll over and go right
to sleep.

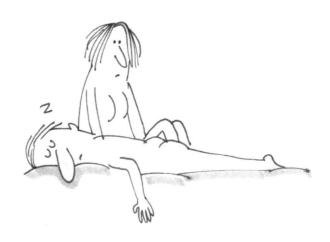

WHY WOMEN HAVE MORE FUN ON THE WEDDING NIGHT

Women can come 26 times and then want to stay up all night talking about love.

WHAT TO DO IF YOU'RE DISAPPOINTED

Sometimes it happens that your first encounter with your new groom is not, shall we say, all that you have read it is supposed to be. Maybe he's a little nervous; maybe he's a little drunk from the wedding; maybe he's a little drunk and a little nervous and a little suicidal.

And what happens is, he can't "perform."

How should you, as a new bride, handle the situation? As with anything, there are good things to do, and there are bad things to do.

GOOD THINGS TO DO
IF YOU'RE DISAPPOINTED

Many experts say there are several things you can do if your new husband is having problems performing.

1. Be a good sport about it. Say to him, "Don't worry about it, honey. We have the rest of our lives to be together."

2. Be kind and understanding. Soothe his brow and say, "There, there. Everything's going to be okay."

3. Be a trooper about it. Sigh quietly, cover him up, and watch him lovingly while he sleeps.

BAD THINGS TO DO
IF YOU'RE DISAPPOINTED

These same experts also say that there are several things you should never do if your husband is having problems performing. They say you should never:

1. Laugh sarcastically and say, "And for this I gave up a perfectly good Saturday night?"

2. Storm off to see "if the guy across the hall is busy."

3. Laugh scornfully and say, "I guess all the guys at the truck stop were right."

BAD THINGS TO DO
IF YOU'RE DISAPPOINTED

4. Snap angrily and say, "Well, hurry it up. I haven't got all night."

5. Drum your fingers impatiently on the night table and keep looking at your watch.

6. Mutter under your breath, "Wimp."

SHOULD YOUR MOTHER STAY IN THE ROOM WITH YOU?

THE PROS AND CONS

There are two schools of thought on this subject: the pro-moms and the anti-moms.

The pro-moms would have you believe that a girl's best friend is her mother, and that best friends stick together in times of need, and there is no greater time of need than when some strange man is chasing you around a bed with intent to make you a vessel for his lust.

SHOULD YOUR MOTHER STAY IN THE ROOM WITH YOU?

The anti-moms would have you believe that you have to be crazy to have your mother with you on your wedding night, for obvious reasons, not to mention how embarrassed you get when the subject of sex is brought up when your mom is in the room.

The pro-moms think it is a girl's duty to be considerate of her mother and not to hurt her feelings by telling her "No."

SHOULD YOUR MOTHER STAY IN THE ROOM WITH YOU?

The anti-moms think only a dipstick would even bring the subject up.

The pro-moms want someone there to hold their hand if it hurts.

The anti-moms prefer to call their lawyer if it hurts.

But you're going to have to decide this for yourself; hey, you're a big girl now.

WHAT FOREPLAY MEANS TO WOMEN

WHAT FOREPLAY MEANS TO MEN

Getting through the list on this page as fast as possible.

Touching   Massaging

Kissing   Sucking

Smiling   Licking

Caressing   Sighing

Undressing

IS IT A GOOD IDEA TO WEAR PAJAMAS?

Let me put it this way. Wearing pajamas to bed on your wedding night is a better idea than wearing a blue serge suit to bed on your wedding night. But it's not very cool.

IS IT A GOOD IDEA TO WEAR PAJAMAS?

What's cool is wearing silk socks to bed on your wedding night.

What's cool is wearing a black cashmere mask to bed on your wedding night.

What's cool is covering yourself with Cool Whip on your wedding night and saying to your new bride, "Ready for dessert?"

What's cool is wearing a cape of feathers to bed on your wedding night and crowing like a rooster every time there is something to crow about.

But pajamas? Frankly, I'd rather go to bed covered with peanut butter (also cool, if it's chunky.)

HOW TO TELL IF YOU'RE GOING TO HAVE A GOOD TIME ON YOUR WEDDING NIGHT

Many grooms ask, "How can I tell if I'm going to have a good time on my wedding night?"

That's a stupid question.

All they have to do is watch for any of the Four Golden Signs. If they see any of the Four Golden Signs, then they know that they are going to have a good time.

WHAT ARE THE FOUR GOLDEN SIGNS?

If you see any of the following, then you have seen one of the Four Golden Signs. If you see:

1. A belly dancing band setting up next to your bed, then you have seen one of the Four Golden Signs.
2. Your bride disappears into the bathroom with a bottle marked, "Atomic Aphrodisiac," then you have seen one of the Four Golden Signs.
3. People gathering in the hall outside your room, whispering, "Hey, you've gotta see this; I understand she's unbelievable," then you have seen one of the Four Golden Signs.
4. Steam rising off your bride's naked hips, then you have seen one of the Four Golden Signs.

GOOD THINGS TO SAY ON YOUR WEDDING NIGHT

Oooh, it's sooo big. Please be gentle.

Certainly I can keep it up all night.

Of course I love you.

I've never done this before (women).

Feel my breasts—that's good—
     harder, harder, slower.

BAD THINGS TO SAY ON YOUR WEDDING NIGHT

Isn't that cute?

I've never done this before (men).

Is $50 O.K.?

I thought it would be, well,
  you know, bigger.

5

GREAT FOREPLAY TECHNIQUES

1. Caress your partner's buttocks with the smooth side of a garlic bagel. (For use of the rough side, see the Kinky Sex Chapter.)

2. Feed each other Maui Potato Chips using only your thighs.

GREAT FOREPLAY TECHNIQUES

3. Undress each other using only your teeth.

4. Spread some chocolate Häagen Daz ice cream over your spouse's erogenous zones. Slowly lick it off. (Don't let the chambermaid see the sheets.)

5. Float your spouse in a warm bath and use a vibrator on any parts that rise above the surface.

THINGS TO SAY
DURING YOUR ORGASM

Aaaaarragh

Yesyesyesyes

OooohAaaahOouch

ImcomingImcomingImcoming

LarryLarryLarry
    (Hopefully your husband's name.)

THINGS TO SAY DURING YOUR SPOUSE'S ORGASM

Are you done yet?

You're hurting me.

You're really hurting me.

You're doing it wrong.

Do you love me?

WHERE DO FEMALE ORGASMS COME FROM?

☐ The vagina
☐ The G-Spot
☐ The Tooth Fairy
☐ A pelvic reaction to screaming obscenities
☐ All of the above.
☐ No one really knows

No one really knows

WHERE DO MALE ORGASMS COME FROM?

All of the above

Talking dirty in locker rooms ☐

Exposing a penis to the air ☐
for more than a few seconds

20 seconds of foreplay ☐

An active fantasy life ☐

A tiny feather implanted ☐
beneath the coccyx that wiggles
during copulation

All of the above ☐

HOW TO TELL IF YOUR HUSBAND HAS HAD AN ORGASM

Your husband, upon orgasm,
will immediately roll over and
fall soundly asleep. Do not
waste your breath talking to him
about love, relationships or true
happiness.

HOW TO TELL IF YOUR WIFE HAS HAD AN ORGASM

You should realize that there is no way a man can really tell when a woman has had an orgasm. All girls are taught, when still very young, secret acting techniques by their friends and mothers. The techniques include screaming, hysterical laughing, hyperventilation and other noises to confound all but the most perceptive males and a few gynecologists. A hoodwinked male can, however, make a few informed observations.

She may have had an orgasm if:

1. She sleeps soundly and snores like a longshoreman.

2. The lubricating jelly has melted into a puddle.

3. She calls you at work 3 times the following day.

4. She says you can come now.

FARTING ON YOUR WEDDING NIGHT

It is very impolite to fart on your wedding night. What ever will your spouse think of you? No, it's better to chance a total explosion of your digestive system than to fart at a time like this.

FARTING ON YOUR WEDDING NIGHT

After the first night, it's perfectly acceptable to fart every now and then, especially if done under the covers. People hold the covers down really tight to try to keep the smell in, but this never works. It's especially foolish to do this if your spouse's head is under the covers.

CONDOMS

Condoms come in only one size, which means they are either very stretchy or all penises are the same size. Putting on a condom is easy provided the man has an erection. Without an erection, it takes several sets of nimble fingers to hold the thing open and one strong hand to stuff with.

CONDOMS

The only real tough part about using condoms is getting the little foil or plastic packages open. There is no way to do this romantically. Most often the package is opened under the covers using teeth and one hand while trying to continue foreplay with the other.

10
GREAT WEDDING NIGHT FANTASIES

1. Tied with leather in the big corral.

2. Cheerleader's shower at Central High.

3. Ice cube tickle with the crotchless panties.

4. Whipped with feathers in the Sultan's Palace.

5. Marooned at sea with 6 Chippendales.

10

GREAT WEDDING NIGHT FANTASIES

6. Spanking naughty coeds.

7. Ravished by the Gaucho Horde.

8. The vibrating enema.

9. Trading clothes in the hotel elevator.

10. Bath time with the new French Maid.

WEIGHT LOSS ON YOUR WEDDING NIGHT

While your wedding night is not the time to worry about your diet, you will find many of the activities have a terrific calorie burning capacity.

ACTIVITY	CALORIES BURNED
Undressing	
a. Undressing alone	25 calories
b. When spouse is laughing at you	225 calories
Removing Bra	
a. If a woman	25 calories
b. If a man	225 calories
c. If a man with one hand	275 calories
Removing Pantyhose	
a. If a woman	22 calories
b. Partially removing pantyhose	205 calories
c. Forgetting to remove pantyhose	575 calories

WEIGHT LOSS ON YOUR WEDDING NIGHT

ACTIVITY	CALORIES BURNED
Sex Fantasies	
a. Talking spouse into fantasy	10 to 350 calories depending
b. Laughing at spouse's fantasy	25 calories
c. Gathering paraphernalia	162 calories
d. Finding pimple on nose	20 calories
e. Finding pimple "down there"	200 calories
f. Forgetting spouse's name	10 calories
g. Hoping spouse will forget your name	100 calories

WEIGHT LOSS ON YOUR WEDDING NIGHT

ACTIVITY	CALORIES BURNED
Using The Toilet Afterwards	
a. Going to the bathroom	50 calories
b. Finding toilet in the dark	75 calories
c. Stepping in champagne bucket	162 calories
d. Peeing in closet by mistake (includes cleanup)	75 calories
e. Sitting on porcelain when seat was lifted up	120 calories
f. Trying to use toilet quietly	420 calories
g. Making cover-up sounds	125 calories

WEIGHT LOSS ON YOUR WEDDING NIGHT

ACTIVITY	CALORIES BURNED
The Morning After	
a. Seeing spouse naked and without makeup	350 calories
b. Finding clothes	25 calories per laugh
c. Not finding clothes	162 calories
d. Acting out fantasy	75 calories
e. Feeling ridiculous	120 calories
f. Convincing spouse not to tell friends	420 calories

GOOD THINGS TO SAY DURING LOVEMAKING

Ooooh, it's so big.

I've never done this before.

No, my tongue never gets tired.

I could keep this up forever.

After they made you, they threw
    away the mold.

Ooooh, it's so tight.

Don't stop.

BAD THINGS TO SAY DURING LOVEMAKING

What's that smell?

Have you ever done this with a sheep?

The doctor said I should be "clean" by now.

Is the toilet close by?

Is it in?

GOOD THINGS TO SAY AFTER LOVEMAKING

You were the best ever.

Yes; six times.

It was so big.

We were so together.

Where am I?

You can come now.

BAD THINGS TO SAY AFTER LOVEMAKING

Are you finished yet?

What did you say your name is?

I guess you haven't had much
    experience with this.

Guess what broke.

Don't think you can just go to sleep now.

You did it wrong.

Just leave it on the dresser.

WHAT TO DO IF SHE REFUSES TO COME OUT OF THE BATHROOM

Sometimes it will happen that the bride will lose her nerve at the last minute and will lock herself in the bathroom until she thinks you have gone to sleep. (Later, when you have been married for a while, this will become so commonplace that it will not bother you anymore.)

Should you try to talk her out of the bathroom, or should you pretend that you have gone to sleep, then jump her when she comes to bed?

Some grooms prefer to talk, saying reassuring things through the bathroom door, making stupid promises that they are never going to be able to keep, ("I'll never love anyone else," or, "Gentle? Of course I'm going to be gentle,") and wondering privately why this is happening to them.

WHAT TO DO IF SHE REFUSES TO COME OUT OF THE BATHROOM

I personally think talking is a waste of energy. You should lie down and conserve your energy for when she comes out of the bathroom and you jump her. Some of those brides are small, but wiry.

Later, when she locks herself back in the bathroom, you can use the free time to go through the wedding gifts looking for cash.

When she comes out of the bathroom, jump her!

WHAT TO DO IF YOU CALL HER BY SOMEONE ELSE'S NAME

Look, it happens sometimes. You will be locked in a passionate embrace, and, lunging toward ecstasy, will scream out, "Oh, Babette, I love you." Needless to say, this will halt your wife, Thelma, in mid-lunge and you will have some heavy explaining to do.

The most important thing is not to panic. Run for your life, yes. But panic, no. Listen to the old master. There are five specific solutions to this specific problem.

WHAT TO DO IF YOU CALL HER BY SOMEONE ELSE'S NAME

FIVE SPECIFIC SOLUTIONS

In this specific situation, there are five specific things which grooms have been doing since the very dawn of time. Unfortunately, only two of them work, but you may get lucky. You can always:

1. Hope she didn't hear you.

2. Pretend you didn't say it.

3. Simply say, "I owe you one."

4. Simply say, "Just kidding."

5. Try changing the subject.

SUPPOSE YOU'RE DRUNK
ON YOUR WEDDING NIGHT

Advantages:

Women can be relaxed enough for great orgasms and men numb enough to go on forever.

You have no guilty feelings, whatever your performance.

You can do things you would never dream of if you were sober.

SUPPOSE YOU'RE DRUNK ON YOUR WEDDING NIGHT

Disadvantages:

You can't remember the good parts.

Your clothes may be strewn in the hotel lobby.

You may be too hung-over to start the next day with a little nookie.

PETS ON YOUR WEDDING NIGHT

Some people are so attached to their pets that they take the animals along on their wedding night. Curious pets can cause more sexual inhibition than the whole Victorian age, flannel nighties and whisker burns put together.

Why Pets Interfere:

1. All pets are curious.

2. Some want to join the fun.

3. Many pets are jealous for the affection.

4. A pet may want to protect its master from what the animal sees as mortal combat.

PETS ON YOUR WEDDING NIGHT

You have 4 choices when trying to handle curious pets:

1. Firmness: "Out, Fido, Out!"

2. Substitution: "I'd like to exchange 'Mom Cat' for a new girlfriend."

3. Bribing: "See the nice bone."

4. Resignation: "Here, Kitty, hold these panties."

KINKY SEX ON YOUR WEDDING NIGHT

Kinky sex will add another dimension to your wedding night fun. Unimaginable pleasures emerge from playing all the games you have ever fantasized about. You have to, of course, talk your partner into these little idiosyncrasies.

TALKING YOUR PARTNER INTO KINKY SEX

1. Talk about it realistically, maturely and with dignity.

2. Calm his or her shrieking or hysterical laughter while you explain why the rubber sheets, zucchini, goldfish and Japanese swing are really necessary for your total fulfillment.

3. Resign yourself to having all your partner's friends refer to you as 'that weirdo' from now on.

KINKY SEX

GOING TOO FAR

It's easy to get carried away with kinky fantasies. You've gone too far when:

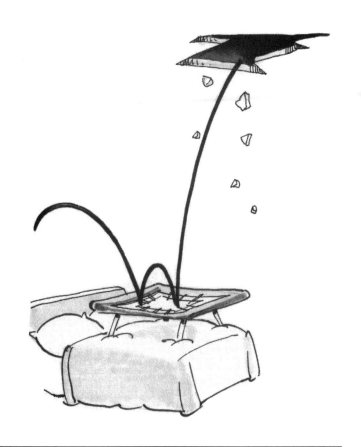

1. Your partner faints.

2. Your partner gags.

3. Your partner slides off the apparatus and into the next room.

4. The hotel staff complain about the goat droppings.

GOING TOO FAR

5. Your partner physically attacks you (unless that is part of your fantasy).

6. The water starts to leak into the lobby.

7. Your tongue gets so swollen that intelligible speech is no longer possible.

KINKY SEX

CALMING A HORRIFIED PARTNER

First, calmly put away the oils, the enemas, the chains and leather, the vibrators and the chicken suits. Then decide which of the 3 guaranteed methods of calming a horrified partner you will use.

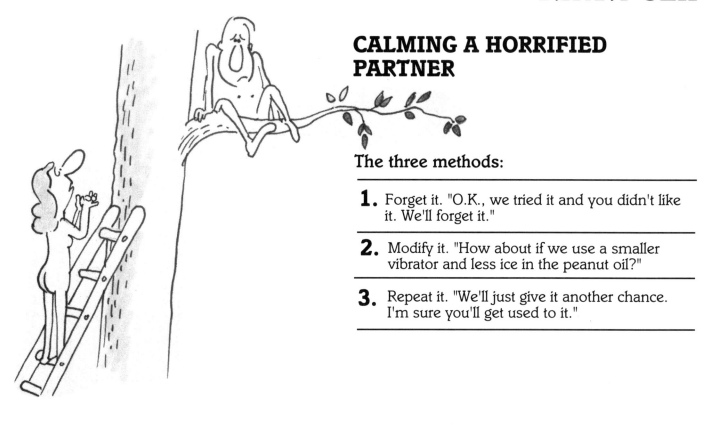

CALMING A HORRIFIED PARTNER

The three methods:

1. Forget it. "O.K., we tried it and you didn't like it. We'll forget it."

2. Modify it. "How about if we use a smaller vibrator and less ice in the peanut oil?"

3. Repeat it. "We'll just give it another chance. I'm sure you'll get used to it."

ADVANCED WEDDING NIGHT ACTIVITY

THE SIMULTANEOUS ORGASM

Simultaneous orgasms are a wonderful goal to work towards on your wedding night. Sort of like a final exam. A few couples find them easy to achieve, but most find the deft sense of timing, the endurance and the delicate balance elusive.

ADVANCED WEDDING NIGHT ACTIVITY

THE SIMULTANEOUS ORGASM

Watch out for people who claim to have simultaneous orgasms all the time. They probably lie about other things as well.

Most people think simultaneous orgasms are not an objective, but more of a miracle.

HONEYMOON COUPLES ASK: SEVEN COMMON QUESTIONS ABOUT THE WEDDING NIGHT

Question #1

How much time should we spend talking and exploring our feelings before we become intimate?

Answer:

It varies from couple to couple, but the average time is about six seconds. You, on the other hand, may prefer to get right down to business. It's all a matter of personal preference.

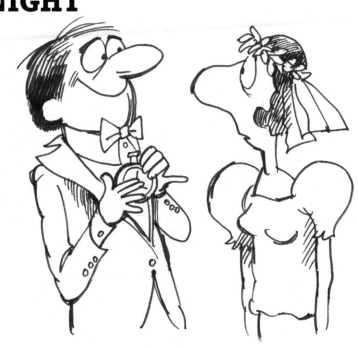

HONEYMOON COUPLES ASK: SEVEN COMMON QUESTIONS ABOUT THE WEDDING NIGHT

Question #2

Who should make the first move?

Answer:

It all depends on who has the greater need.

Question #3

How will we know who has the greater need?

Answer:

It will be the one who makes the first move.

HONEYMOON COUPLES ASK: SEVEN COMMON QUESTIONS ABOUT THE WEDDING NIGHT

Question #4

If someone knocks at the door while we are making love, should we answer it?

Answer:

Only if it's someone with oxygen.

Question #5

What if, after we get into bed together, we discover that we don't turn each other on?

Answer:

Welcome to the club.

HONEYMOON COUPLES ASK: SEVEN COMMON QUESTIONS ABOUT THE WEDDING NIGHT

Question #6

When should we call our parents?

Answer:

Later, when you run out of money.

Question #7

When is it all right to shower together?

Answer:

When you have taken off all your clothes.

WHAT IF HE WANTS TO TAKE PICTURES?

Three Memorable Wedding Night Poses

Sometimes grooms get sentimental and decide that they want to have a picture of you on your wedding night so that they can remember it forever and ever.

This is very touching (until later, when you realize they only want the picture to show their buddies what a terrific body you have,) and you will probably want to make him happy by posing.

But what pose to take? As photo amateurs, you will probably waste precious hours of your wedding night trying different poses till you get the one that is best.

Let me save you some time. Here are three wedding night poses you can use that will give you a lasting memory you will never erase.

WHAT IF HE WANTS TO TAKE PICTURES?

POSE #1:

POSE #2:

POSE #3:

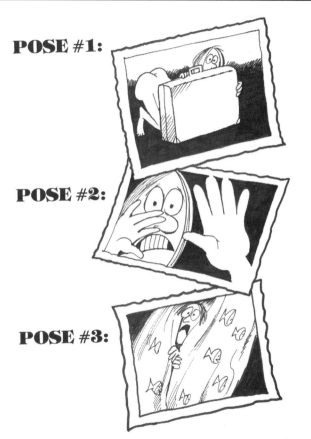

WEDDING NIGHT PROBLEMS

FAILURE TO ACHIEVE ORGASM

The most common reasons for failure to achieve orgasm are:

1. Not in the mood.
2. Incompetent foreplay.
3. Bellman refuses to leave.
4. Bellman refuses to stay.

WEDDING NIGHT PROBLEMS

FAILURE TO ACHIEVE ORGASM

5. Partner not really trying.

6. Partner has moustache and you are a man.

7. Partner wears bra and you are a woman.

WEDDING NIGHT PROBLEMS

FRIGIDITY

The 6 main causes of frigidity in women are:

1. Partner asks how long you are going to take.

2. Partner calls you by wrong name.

3. You think you hear someone's kids or your parents at door.

WEDDING NIGHT PROBLEMS

FRIGIDITY

4. Partner confesses to being gay.

5. You're afraid of someone coming into the room, especially your old boyfriend.

6. Partner's religious medallion keeps bashing you in the nose.

RATING YOUR SPOUSE

A Good Spouse

A good spouse doesn't ask how are you doing, but kisses you before falling asleep, volunteers to sleep on the wet spot and is not disturbed by loud farting.

RATING YOUR SPOUSE

A Bad Spouse

A bad spouse has cold hands and feet, keeps TV on so as not to waste time, knows only 2 positions and moves only to go to the bathroom.

HOW TO HANDLE ALL THE GAWKING STARES THE NEXT MORNING AT BREAKFAST

Usually, the worst part of the honeymoon comes at breakfast following your wedding night when you walk into the hotel restaurant and all the people turn around to stare at you as if to say, "We know what **you've** been doing."

Many a bride has spent that breakfast brushing tears off her poached eggs, while grooms pretend not to notice and eat like fullbacks instead.

This is a very delicate situation, and unless you know how to defuse it, it can explode in your face, leaving you with deep and lasting emotional scars.

HOW TO HANDLE ALL THE GAWKING STARES THE NEXT MORNING AT BREAKFAST

How To Defuse It

1. Pretend it is not happening.

2. Pretend that it is happening but that you do not care.

3. Pretend that you and your husband have been married for 18 years, not 18 hours, and that all the screaming, panting, groaning and squealing coming from your room all night was nothing unusual.

HOW TO HANDLE ALL THE GAWKING STARES THE NEXT MORNING AT BREAKFAST

Anything else you do is only going to make it worse. You may think that it will help, but it will not help if you:

1. Go from table to table claiming, "Nothing happened, really. We just stayed up all night and talked."

2. Go from table to table claiming, "It's all right. We're married. See the ring."

3. Stand up on your table and scream, "Yes, yes, we did it! And it was great! Now are you happy?"

WEDDING NIGHT DIARY

	Time	How Long It Lasted
We did it for the first time at		
We did it for the second time at		
We did it for the third time at		
We did it for the fourth time at		
We did it for the fifth time at		
We did it for the sixth time at		
We did it for the seventh time at		
We did it for the eighth time at		
We did it for the ninth time at		
We did it for the tenth time at		
We did it for the eleventh time at		
We did it for the twelfth time at		
We did it for the thirteenth time at		
We did it for the fourteenth time at		
We did it for the fifteenth time at		

WEDDING NIGHT COMMANDMENTS

I. Thou shalt not skimp on foreplay.

II. Thou shalt indulge your spouse's fantasies, no matter how idiotic.

III. Thou shalt not climax before your spouse.

IV. Thou shalt engage in at least a little afterplay before falling asleep.

V. Thou shalt encourage your spouse to reach multiple orgasms.

WEDDING NIGHT COMMANDMENTS

VI. Thou shalt not make fun of your spouse's insufficiencies.

VII. Thou shalt not make faces during oral sex.

VIII. Thou shalt endure excruciatingly uncomfortable positions if they really make your spouse happy.

IX. Thou shalt search diligently for erogenous zones.

X. Thou shalt not speak about your experiences with anyone but your best friend.

Other books we publish are available at many fine stores. If you can't find them, send directly to us. $7.00 postpaid

2400-How To Have Sex On Your Birthday. Finding a partner, special birthday sex positions and much more.

2402-Confessions From The Bathroom. There are things in this book that happen to all of us that none of us ever talk about, like the Gas Station Dump, the Corn Niblet Dump and more.

2403-The Good Bonking Guide. Great new term for doing "you know what". Bonking in the dark, bonking all night long, improving your bonking, and everything else you ever wanted to know.

2407-40 Happens. When being out of prune juice ruins your whole day and you realize anyone with the energy to do it on a weeknight must be a sex maniac.

2408-30 Happens. When you take out a lifetime membership at your health club, and you still wonder when the baby fat will finally disappear.

2409-50 Happens. When you remember when "made in Japan" meant something that didn't work, and you can't remember what you went to the top of the stairs for.

2411-The Geriatric Sex Guide. It's not his mind that needs expanding; and you're in the mood now, but by the time you're naked, you won't be!

2412-Golf Shots. What excuses to use to play through first, ways to distract your opponent, and when and where a true golfer is willing to play.

2416-The Absolutely Worst Fart Book. The First Date Fart, The Lovers' Fart, The Doctor's Exam Room Fart and more.

2417-Women Over 30 Are Better Because... Their nightmares about ex-ams are starting to fade and their handbags can sustain life for about a week with no outside support whatsoever.

2418-9 Months In The Sac. Pregnancy through the eyes of the baby, such as: why do pregnant women have to go to the bathroom as soon as they get to the store, and why does baby start doing aerobics when it's time to sleep?

2419-Cucumbers Are Better Than Men Because... Cucumbers are always ready when you are and cucumbers will never hear "yes, yes" when you're saying "NO, NO."

2421-Honeymoon Guide. The Advantages Of Undressing With The Light On (it's easier to undo a bra) to What Men Want Most (being able to sleep right afterwards and not talk about love).

2422-Eat Yourself Healthy. Calories only add up if the food is consumed at a table and green M&M's are full of the same vitamins found in broccoli.

2423-Is There Sex After 40? She liked you better when the bulge above your waist was in your trousers. He thinks wife-swapping means getting someone else to cook for you.

2424-Is There Sex After 50? Going to bed early means a chance to catch up on your reading and you miss making love quietly so as not to wake the kids.

2425-Women Over 40 Are Better Because... No matter how many sit-ups they do, they can't recapture their 17-year-old body—but they can find something attractive in any 21-year-old guy.

2426-Women Over 50 Are Better Because... They will be amused if you take them parking, and they know that being alone is better than being with someone they don't like.

2427-You Know You're Over The Hill When... All your stories have bored most acquaintances several times over. You're resigned to being overweight after trying every diet that has come along in the last 15 years.

2428-Beer Is Better Than Women Because (Part II)... A beer doesn't get upset if you call it by the wrong name; and after several beers, you can go to sleep without having to talk about love.

2429-Married To A Computer. You fondle it daily, you keep in touch when you're travelling and you stare at it a lot without understanding it.

2430-Is There Sex After 30? He thinks foreplay means parading around nude in front of the mirror, holding his stomach in; and she found that the quickest way to get rid of a date is to start talking about commitment.

2431-Happy Birthday You Old Fart! You spend less and less time between visits to a toilet, your back goes out more than you do and you leave programming the VCR to people under 25.

2432-Big Weenies. Why some people have big weenies while other people have teenie weenies; as well as the kinds of men who possess a member, a rod and a wang—and more!

2433-Games You Can Play With Your Pussy. Why everyone should have a pussy; how to give a pussy a bath (grease the sides of the tub so it can't claw its way out); and more!

2434-Sex And Marriage. What wives want out of marriage–romance, respect and a Bloomingdale's chargecard; what husbands want out of marriage –to be allowed to sleep after sex.

2435-Baby's First Year. How much will it cost, secrets of midnight feedings, do diapers really cause leprosy and other vital info for parents.

2436-How To Love A New Yorker. You love a New Yorker by pretending to understand their accent, sharing a parking space and realizing they look at "Out of Towners" as new income.

2437-The Retirement Book. Updates the retiree on Early Bird Specials, finding their bifocals and remembering things like paying for the book.

2438-Dog Farts. They do it under the table, in front of the TV, and after devouring some animal they caught in the yard. This book describes them all.

2439-Handling His Midlife Crisis. By treating him like a child when he wants to feel young again and consoling him when he goes from bikinis to boxer shorts.

2440-How To Love A Texan. You love a Texan by agreeing that their chili is just a mite hot, humoring them when they refer to their half acre as a ranch and rushing to help when their belt buckle sets off a security alarm.

2441-Bedtime Stories for your Kitty. Kitties love a story before bedtime and this book guarantees to keep their attention; Goldisocks and the 3 Teddy Bears, The 3 Little Kittens, and more.

2442-Bedtime Stories for your Doggie. This book of tales will keep big doggies as well as puppies entranced every night with stories like The 3 Billy Dogs Gruff, The Little Doggie That Could and many more.

2443-60 With Sizzle! When your kids start to look middle-aged and when your hearing is perfect if everyone would just stop mumbling.

Ivory Tower Publishing Co., Inc., 125 Walnut St., P.O. Box 9132, Watertown, MA 02272-9132   Tel: (617) 923-1111